Gwen Ma[...]

# Needlework
# DESIGNS

**American Quilter's Society**
P. O. Box 3290 • Paducah, KY 42002-3290
www.AmericanQuilter.com

# Acknowledgments

I thank Pat Holly, Deb Ballard, Carol Grossman, Sharon Finton, Mary Hovey, Laureen Searing, and Pat Anisko for the use of their quilts in this book. These women are friends of many years who have long supported my efforts and have enriched my life in many ways. It is to them that I dedicate this book.

This is the sixth book I've published with the American Quilter's Society and I thank the company and editorial staff for their helpful guidance and encouragement.

Located in Paducah, Kentucky, the American Quilter's Society (AQS) is dedicated to promoting the accomplishments of today's quilters. Through its publications and events, AQS strives to honor today's quiltmakers and their work and to inspire future creativity and innovation in quiltmaking.

Editor: Shelley Hawkins
Graphic Design: Elaine Wilson
Illustrations: Lynda Smith
Cover Design: Michael Buckingham
Photography: Charles R. Lynch

Additional copies of this book may be ordered from the American Quilter's Society, PO Box 3290, Paducah, KY 42002-3290; 800-626-5420 (orders only please); or online at www.AmericanQuilter.com. For all other inquiries, call 270-898-7903.

Library of Congress Cataloging-in-Publication Data
Marston, Gwen.
    Gwen Marston's needlework designs / by Gwen Marston.
        p.cm.
    Summary: "Over 75 designs inspired by sixteenth- and seventeenth-century Renaissance and Baroque styles. Motifs can be hand or machine quilted, embroidered, appliqued, or stenciled"--Provided by publisher.
    ISBN 1-57432-898-0
    1. Quilting--Design.  2. Appliqué--Design.  3. Decoration and ornament, Baroque.  4. Decoration and ornament, Renaissance.  I. Title.

    TT835.M27237 2006
    746.4041--dc22
                2005028251

*Proudly printed and bound in the United States of America*

**Cover Quilts:** FRIENDSHIP BOUQUET by Deb Ballard, Sharon Finton, Carol Grossman, Mary Hovey, and Laureen Searing. Hand quilted by the author (page 18). FLOWERS AND STARS by Pat Anisko (page 8).

# Contents

# Introduction

Fanciful, organic shapes that were common in many parts of the world in the sixteenth and seventeenth centuries inspired this collection of designs. Similar designs were part of an everyday vocabulary utilized by craftspeople working in different media. They are seen in early bed rugs, quilts, embroidered bed curtains and bedcovers, tapestries, silver utensils, hand-painted kitchenware, architectural details, and Persian carpets.

My interest in quilting designs began in the mid-1970s when I learned to quilt from a group of Mennonite women in Hubbard, Oregon. Shortly thereafter I met Mary Schafer, a pioneer of the great American quilting revival, who made her large antique quilt collection available to me for study. Mary fanned the fire and I've been searching for motifs that could be used for quilting designs ever since, resulting in this collection. While I use these designs as hand quilting designs, they can also be used by machine quilters, appliqué artists, and redwork enthusiasts.

For many years, I've enjoyed teaching classes about drafting quilting designs to fit specific spaces. This is my fourth quilting design book.

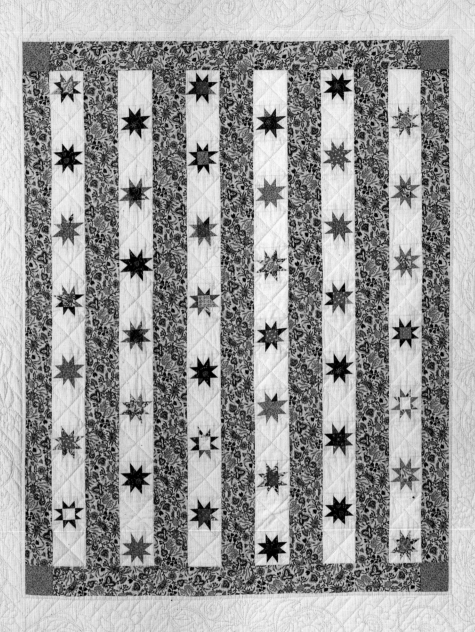

**Little Liberated Stars,** 53" x 62". Designed, made, and hand quilted by the author. In this old-fashioned strippy setting, little 3" finished stars were lined up in long vertical rows separated by wholecloth bars. The border was quilted with a continuous vine from which 23 different floral designs grow. Using a variety of designs adds subtle interest to a quilt. For one who notices and takes the time to really look, there is a series of delightful surprises to discover. See pages 23, 26, 28, 30–32, 34, 36, and 51–65 for the patterns in this quilt.

# How to Use These Designs

These classical designs have multiple applications, as has historically been the case. They can be used for hand and machine quilting, appliqué, embroidery, and stenciling. Their adaptability allows for adjustments. They can be enlarged, rearranged, and used as block or border designs.

They were used as hand quilting patterns in my NINE-PATCH VARIATION (page 14) and LITTLE LIBERATED STARS (page 5) quilts. The Nine-Patch quilt has a different design in each plain block and side triangle. The star quilt makes use of many different designs strung together on a continuous-vine border.

The irregularity and flexibility of these designs make them especially suitable for machine quilting, as Pat Holly so ably illustrates in her fabulous bird quilt (page 7). Deb Ballard, Sharon Finton, Carol Grossman, Mary Hovey, and Laureen Searing selected their favorites from this collection and made the spirited appliqué sampler FRIENDSHIP BOUQUET (page 18). Pat Anisko embroidered 12 of her favorite designs, set them together with liberated star sashing, and made a lovely redwork quilt (page 8).

**Checkerboard Chicks,** 44" x 44". Machine appliquéd and quilted by Pat Holly. A bevy of fun bird appliqué shapes are surrounded by Gwen's quilting designs. The birds are Pat's original designs. The quilting was done with contrasting thread on a home sewing machine. Pat is among those who have helped make machine work so widely recognized and well received today. In this quilt, she highlights how well these designs adapt to free-motion machine quilting. See pages 24 and 45–50 for the patterns in this quilt.

**FLOWERS AND STARS,** 37½" x 48". Made and hand quilted by Pat Anisko. Pat embroidered the blocks with variegated floss and set them together with star sashing. She enjoys embroidery, and she worked on this quilt in the fall and early winter. The stars shone so bright on some of these evenings that Pat decided to add Gwen's liberated stars in the sashing. See pages 23, 26, and 35–44 for the patterns in this quilt.

# Inspiring Your Own Designs

Whether you are quilting, appliquéing, embroidering, or stenciling, you can use these shapes as inspiration for creating your own designs. Fashioning original designs is satisfying and easier than you think. Experiment with this concept. For example, find a floral shape you like and draw something similar. It won't be the same, and that's the idea. It will be your version, just as these drawings are my versions of shapes I've seen. Add a stem, find a leaf shape you like, and refine the design to your satisfaction.

Claiming not to be an artist is no excuse. The majority of the antique quilts we admire were made by women with little or no education, and even fewer with any kind of formal art education. If the idea of drawing is intimidating, don't think of it as drawing, think of it as doodling. I think you will be surprised at how well you do!

# Adjusting the Designs for Quilting

This collection is ideal for quilting designs. Quilting designs look best when they fill the area, which means you may need to adjust them to fit your quilt properly. Copy machines make this an easy task. If you need a design to fill a small area, simplify the design by selecting just part of it and eliminating other parts.

The scale of these designs fits perfectly in the alternate plain blocks of my pink NINE-PATCH VARIATION (page 14), but I had to alter the design I wanted to use in the side and corner triangles (see page 10).

I adjusted block designs to use them as border designs on my LITTLE LIBERATED STARS quilt (page 5). To accomplish this, I

drew a continuous vine freehand directly onto the quilt top, which is the way I've done it for years. It's quick, easy, and I like the look of a freehand-drawn vine meandering along in a naturalistic fashion. Once the vine was drawn all the way around the border, I slipped the floral patterns under the quilt, traced the organic shapes I wanted to use, and drew new stems to connect them to the vine. The whole design rarely fit, so I chose just the part that would work. This myriad of fanciful, organic designs produces a dramatic visual effect, well worth the effort of hand quilting.

# Adapting the Designs
# for Appliqué

FRIENDSHIP BOUQUET, page 18, was made by a group of my friends with designs from this collection. They used the designs the exact size shown in this book and did a beautiful job.

If some of the designs in this collection seem too small to appliqué easily, you can enlarge them. Again, the easiest way to change the size of a design is to use a copy machine. You can also simplify the patterns by ignoring the tiny parts and details. Some designs have single-line tendrils, for example. You can ignore them or include them. One way to handle thin lines is to make thin bias. Another way is to embroider them.

# Tips on Marking Quilts

My first lesson in marking quilts was with my Mennonite teachers. They marked quilts the way they had for the past hundred-plus years: with a lead pencil. According to them, a #2 soft-lead pencil made too dark of a line and could also smudge. Instead, they suggested a #3 or #4 hard-lead pencil, explaining that it left a light, fine line that virtually disappeared when quilted.

Soon after my initial lesson, I perused a stationery and art supply store to explore other possibilities. I found a pencil made by Berol® that had been designed specifically for architects. On the edge of the pencil it read, "Ideal for marking blueprints." For a brief moment, I actually wondered if it would also work on red prints. I'd like to say that I came to my senses quickly. I bought a white and a silver Berol Verithin® pencil and found that both work very well for marking quilts.

I even called the company to inquire about its product and learned a bit more about pencils than I'd previously known. They told me not to use a red pencil for marking my quilts because red pencils were designed specifically not to come out. It seems that during World War II, important reports requiring signatures to be checked off required a permanent pencil that couldn't be altered, and the red pencil came into being. Schoolteachers quickly discovered that this pencil was good insurance against children changing the grade on their homework papers. So stay away from red pencils, and yellow pencils as well, because they respond in a similar way.

I recommend either a hard-lead pencil or a Berol Verithin silver pencil for marking on white fabric or light prints, and a white or silver pencil for marking on dark fabrics. Because there is still uncertainty about how chemical markers perform, I choose not to use them, especially when I have other options that work well.

If you have a light-colored quilt, you can slip the pattern underneath and see it well enough to trace. Darken the lines on the pattern with a black felt-tip pen to make the design easy to see. If you are marking on dark fabric, use a light table.

To make tracing easy, fast, and successful, relax your hand when tracing the patterns. Think of the pattern as just a guide when you draw. If you try to copy the patterns perfectly, you are apt to hold the pencil too tightly, making the work tedious. There is absolutely no benefit in exact reproduction. Close is good in this case and a little variation matters not in the least. Mother Nature constantly reminds us of that fact.

# Quilt Projects

### NINE-PATCH VARIATION

Designed, made, and hand quilted by the author.

Gwen Marston's **Needlework Designs** ⋯⋯⋯⋯⋯⋯⋯⋯⋯⋯⋯⋯⋯⋯⋯⋯⋯⋯⋯⋯⋯⋯

# Nine-Patch Variation

**Quilt Size: 60" x 71"**
**Block Size: 8"**

Each alternate plain block was quilted with a different design, with yet another design quilted in the side triangles. The border was quilted with triple diagonals, reminiscent of quilts from the nineteenth century and far less used by twentieth-century quiltmakers. This unusual variation on the ever-popular Nine-Patch block was formed with four Nine-Patches, separated by split sashing. Reverse color in two of the four Nine-Patch units that make up the block gives this quilt a different appearance.

## Fabric Requirements

*(All pieces are cut from selvage to selvage, except borders, binding, and corner squares, which are cut parallel to the selvage.)*

| Fabric | Yards | Cut |
|---|---|---|
| **Cream** | 3¾ | |
| Outer border | | 2 strips 10" x 55" |
| | | 2 strips 10" x 62½" |
| Side triangles | | 3 squares 6⅝", cut twice diagonally |
| Corner triangles | | 2 squares 12⅝", cut once diagonally |
| Solid blocks | | 6 squares 8½" |
| Nine-Patch blocks | | 14 strips 1½" x 42" |
| **Double Pink*** | 2⅛ | |
| Binding | | 7 strips 2½" x 48" |
| Inner border | | 2 strips 4" x 48" |
| | | 2 strips 4" x 43½" |
| Nine-Patch blocks | | 14 strips 1½" x 42" |
| Corner squares | | 18 squares 1½" (for plain blocks and corner and side triangles) |
| **Batting** | 64" x 75" | |
| **Backing** | 3¾ | |

* NINE-PATCH VARIATION contains 10 different double-pink prints. Yardage and cutting instructions reflect a strip-piecing method of assembly with only one fabric; however, strip-sets made from different fat quarters can be used to make the units in the blocks if a scrap look is desired.

# Nine-Patch Variation

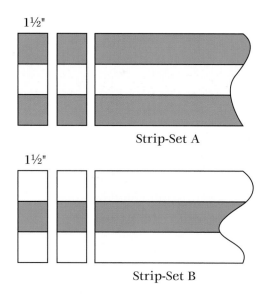

Fig. 1. Strip-sets A and B assembly

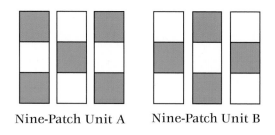

Nine-Patch Unit A    Nine-Patch Unit B

Fig. 2. Nine-Patch units A and B assembly

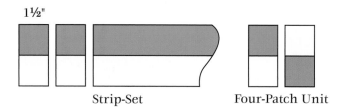

Strip-Set        Four-Patch Unit

Fig. 3. Four-Patch unit assembly

## Nine-Patch Blocks

*1.* To make the Nine-Patch units, join one cream and two double-pink strips as shown to make three of strip-set A. Then, join one double-pink and two cream strips to make three of strip-set B. Cut the strip-sets 1½" apart to make 72 A and 72 B segments (fig. 1).

*2.* Assemble the segments as shown to form 24 of Nine-Patch unit A and 24 of Nine-Patch unit B (fig. 2).

*3.* To make the Four-Patch units, join one cream and one double-pink strip as shown to make one strip-set. Cut the strip-set 1½" apart to make 24 segments. Assemble the segments as shown to make 12 Four-Patch units (fig. 3).

*4.* To make the sashing units, join one cream and one double-pink strip as shown in figure 3 to make four strip-sets. Cut the strip-sets 3½" apart to make 48 sashing units.

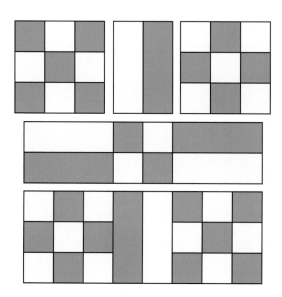

Fig. 4. Nine-Patch block assembly

*5.* Join four Nine-Patch units, one Four-Patch unit, and four sashing units to assemble a Nine-Patch block (fig. 4, page 16). Make 12 Nine-Patch blocks.

## Quilt Assembly

*1.* The Nine-Patch blocks are set on point. For a connected look between them, a double-pink square is added to the center side triangles and solid blocks. To achieve this, appliqué two sides of the corner squares to the tip of six side triangles and to two opposing corners of the six solid blocks with a ¼" turn-under allowance (fig. 5).

*2.* Refer to the quilt assembly diagram to join the Nine-Patch blocks, solid blocks, side triangles, and corner triangles in diagonal rows.

*3.* To ensure the borders will lie flat, measure the quilt from top to bottom and trim the inner side borders to this measurement. Pin both ends and the middle of the borders to the sides of the quilt. Continue pinning the border by dividing the halves repeatedly, pinning every 3". Sew the side borders to the quilt, then repeat this process for the top and bottom borders. Sew the outer borders to the quilt in the same manner.

*4.* Layer the quilt top, batting, and backing. Quilt the layers. The patterns used in this quilt are on pages 23–29. Attach the binding to the quilt.

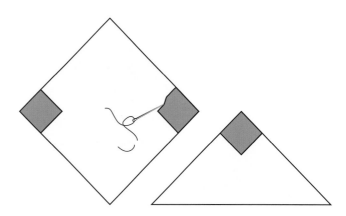

**Fig. 5.** Appliqué the corner squares.

Quilt assembly

## FRIENDSHIP BOUQUET

Made by Deb Ballard, Sharon Finton, Carol Grossman, Mary Hovey, and Laureen Searing.
Hand quilted by the author.

# Friendship Bouquet

**Quilt Size: 45" x 45"**
**Block Size: 9"**

Gwen's friends chose their favorite designs and appliquéd the beautiful blocks in this quilt. They also made their own version of a Dogtooth border. Laureen made the Nine-Patch blocks and Deb assembled the top.

Dogtooth borders, like the ones on this quilt, are appliquéd rather than pieced. These were popular on quilts during the eighteenth and early nineteenth centuries. They are characterized by slight inconsistencies due to the fact that they were cut from lengths of folded fabric. These very inconsistencies give them their charm and differentiate them from their pieced Sawtooth sisters.

The quiltmakers designed their own Dogtooth borders without conferring with each other so they would all be different. The strip width, number of folds, and angle of the cut all affect the end result. The variations add dramatically to the folk art feeling in this delightful charmer.

Gwen drew the feather quilting design freehand on the border of the quilt. This unique design is exceptionally flexible. It can change its size and shape to fill even unpredictable areas, such as the space between the points of the Dogtooth border. The pattern consists of the following variations: continuous feathers that are hooked together, individual feathers, and pointed feathers. The very occasional use of the coiled feather is an elegant idea from the grand tradition of Welsh quilting.

## Fabric Requirements
*(Cut from selvage to selvage)*

| Fabric | Yards | Cut |
|---|---|---|
| **Cream** | 2⅛ | |
| Border | | 4 strips 9½" x 27½" |
| | | 4 squares 9½" |
| Solid blocks | | 5 squares 9½" |
| Binding | | 6 strips 2½" x 42" |
| **Burgundy** | ½ | |
| Dogtooth border | | 4 strips 3½" x 27½" |
| **Medium and dark print** | scraps | |
| Nine-Patch blocks | | 14 medium squares 3½" |
| | | 19 dark squares 3½" |
| **Assorted prints** | scraps | |
| Appliqué | | pattern pages 30–34 |
| **Batting** | 49" x 49" | |
| **Backing** | 3 | |

# Friendship Bouquet

## Block Assembly

*1.* To make a Nine-Patch block, join four medium and five dark print squares as shown. Make two more Nine-Patch blocks in this fashion. For a scrappy look, assemble the fourth block with five medium and four dark print squares (fig. 1).

*2.* With the assorted print scraps, appliqué the patterns listed in the chart or other patterns of your choice on the five solid cream blocks.

## Dogtooth Border

*1.* Fold the burgundy fabric strips in half, or thirds, repeatedly. Experiment to get the width you want for the Dogtooth.

*2.* Practice cutting a folded piece of paper first to make sure you get the look you want. Then, cut a peak on the folded fabric as shown (fig. 2). Repeat for the remaining three borders.

*3.* Appliqué a cut Dogtooth border to each of the cream border strips.

## Quilt Assembly

*1.* Arrange the Nine-Patch blocks and appliquéd blocks in three rows of three as shown in the quilt assembly diagram. Sew the blocks together for each row, then sew the rows together.

*2.* Sew a 9½" border square to each end of two border strips. Sew the border strips without the end squares to the top and bottom of the quilt, then sew the border strips with pieced squares to the sides of the quilt.

*3.* Layer the quilt top, batting, and backing. Quilt the layers. The feather border pattern is on page 21. Attach the binding to the quilt.

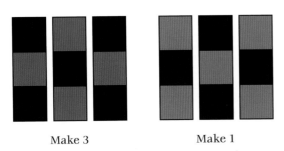

Make 3       Make 1

**Fig. 1.** Nine-Patch block assembly

**Fig. 2.** Cutting the Dogtooth border

Quilt assembly

# Friendship Bouquet
**Border Quilting Design**

Pattern repeat

Pattern repeat

# Patterns

Gwen Marston's **Needlework Designs** ··········································································

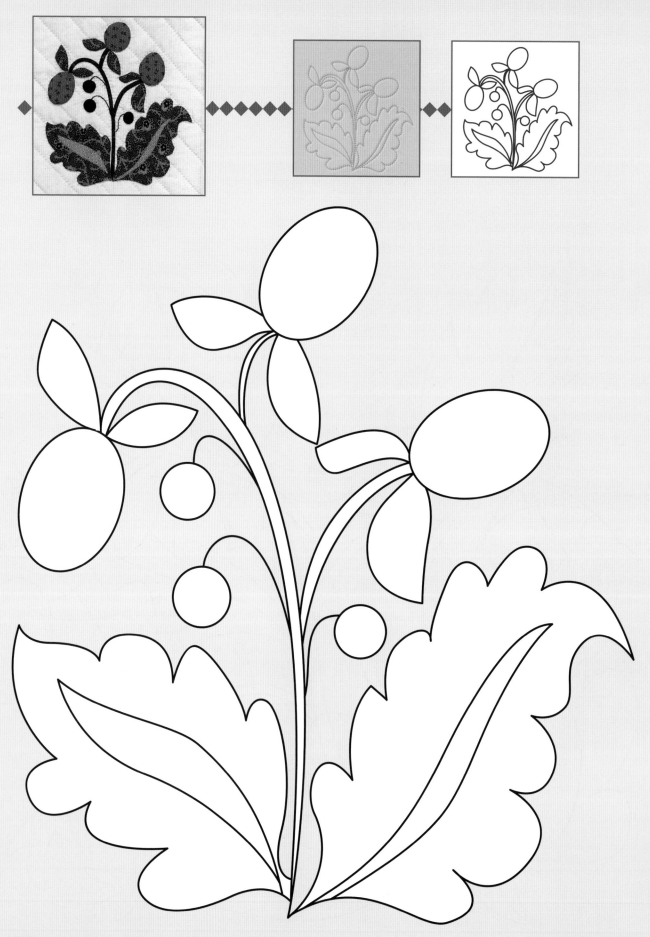

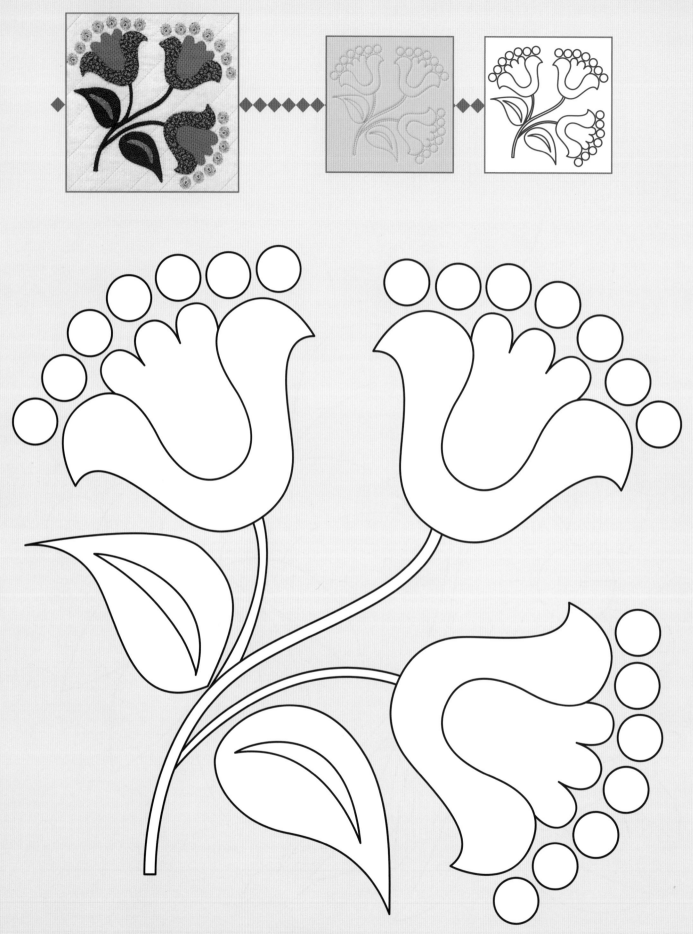

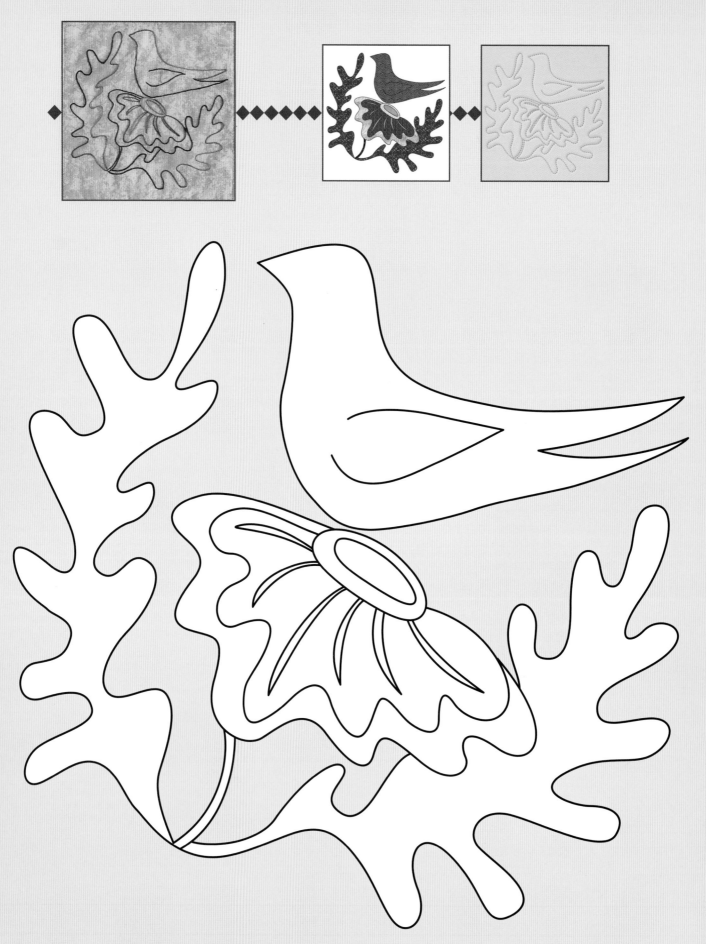

Gwen Marston's Needlework Designs

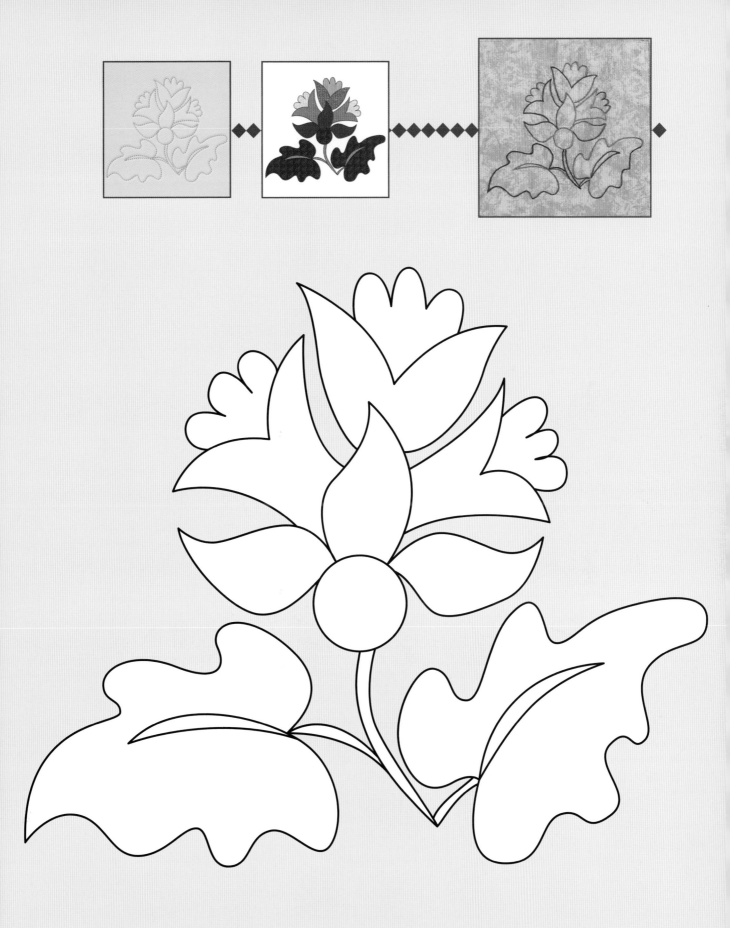

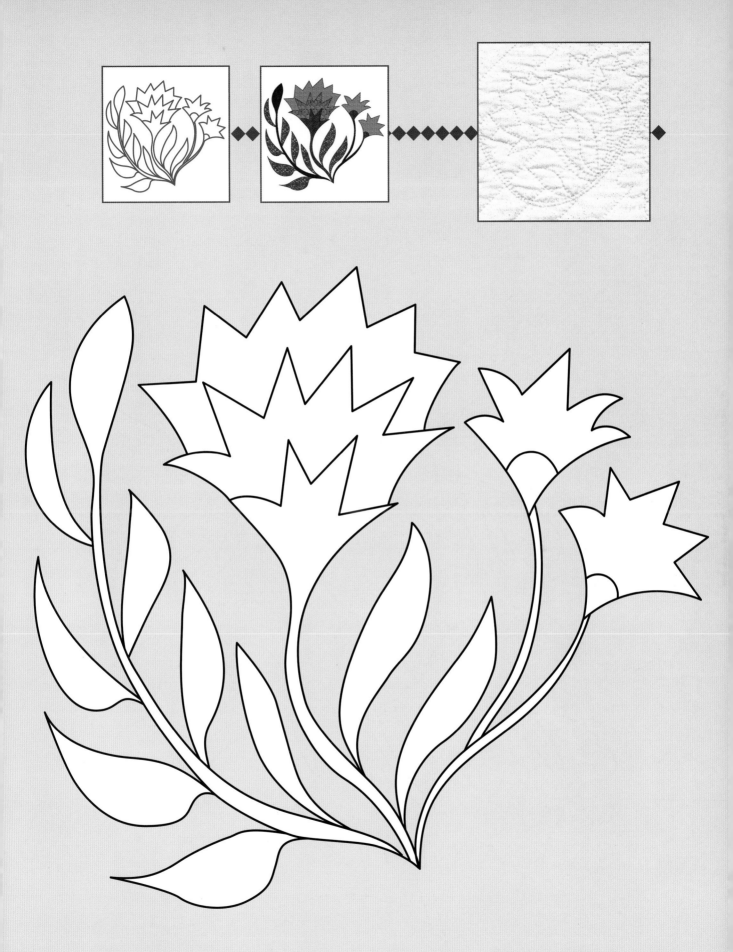

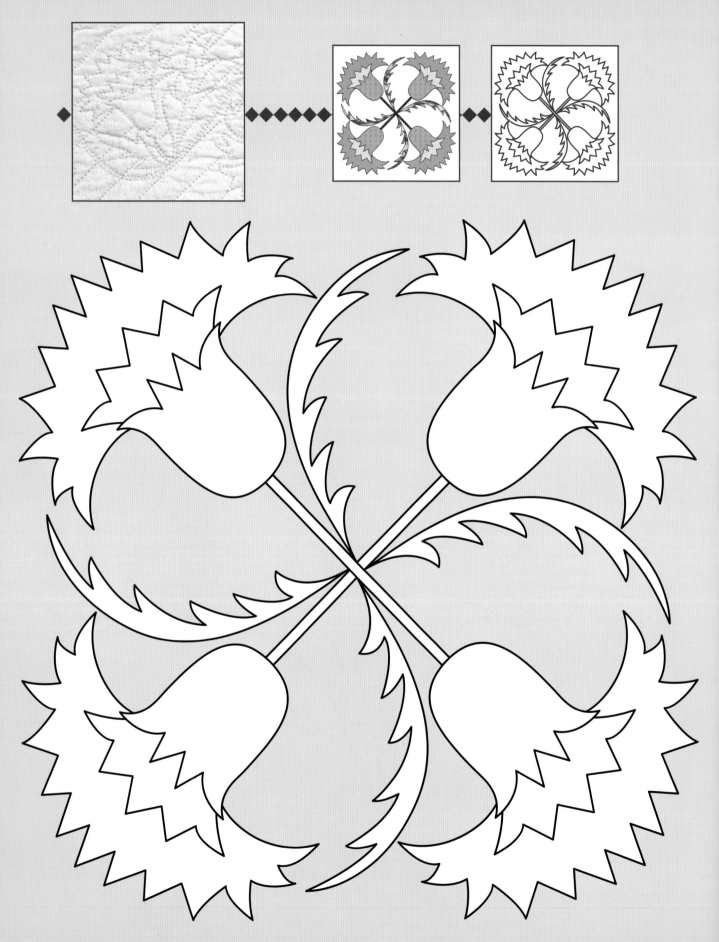

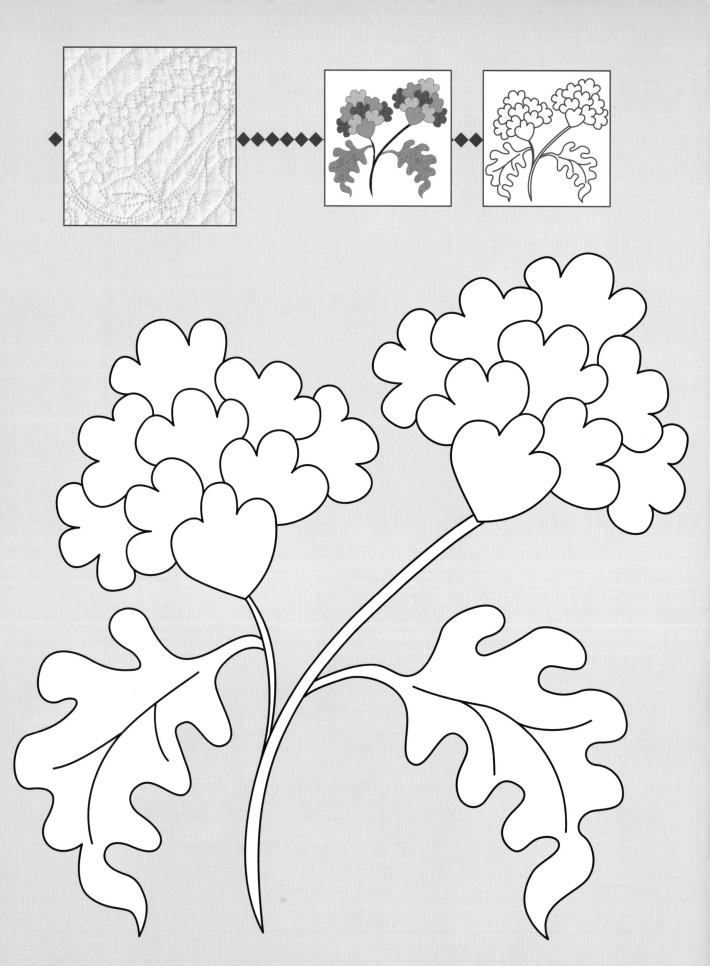

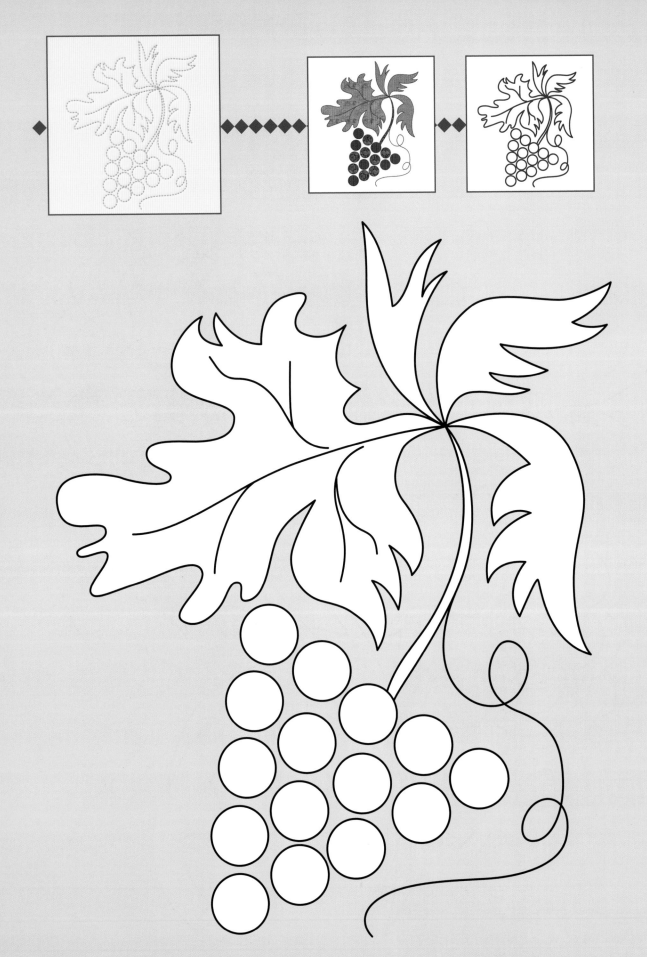

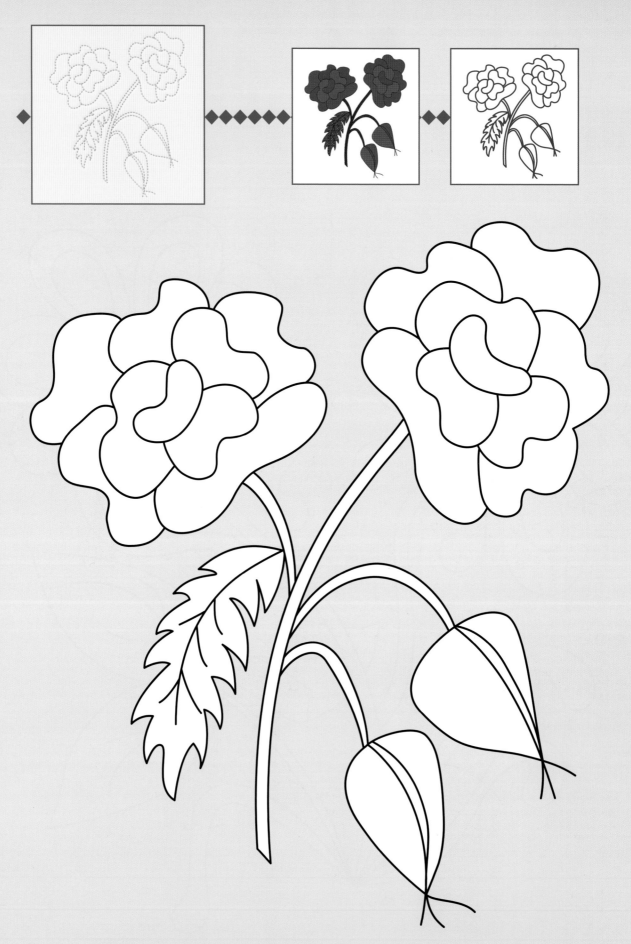

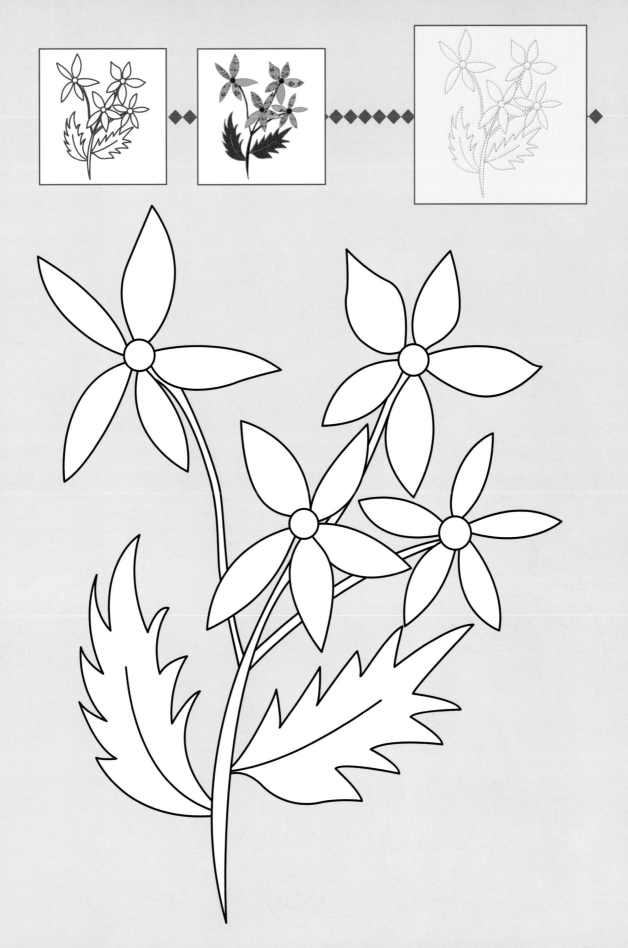

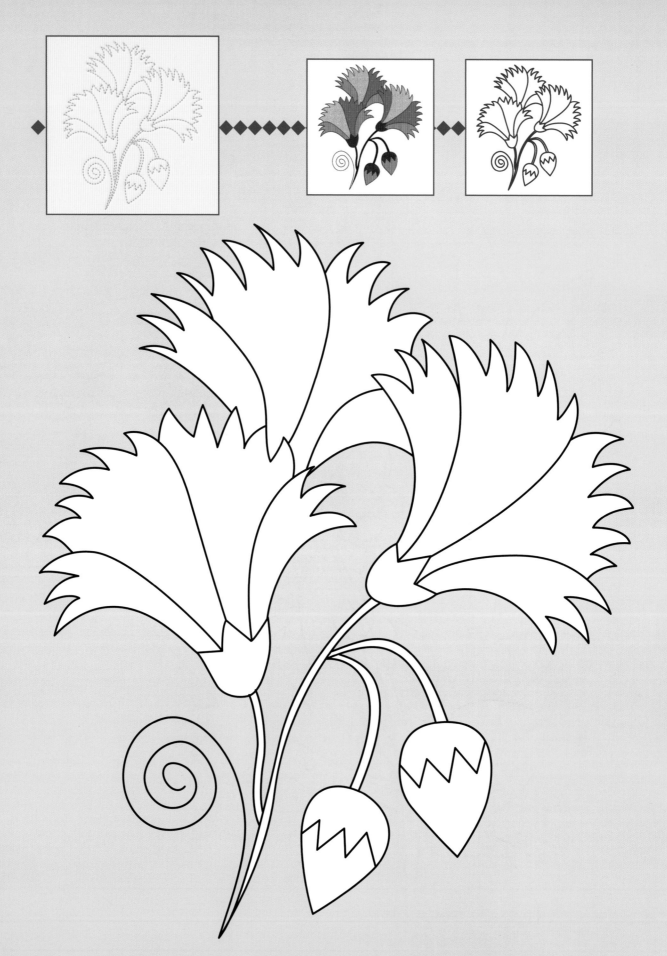

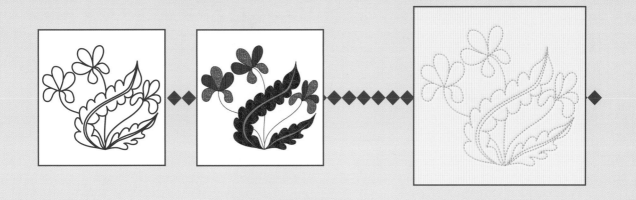

# About the Author

Gwen Marston is a professional quiltmaker, teacher, and author. Since 1981, she has had 19 solo exhibits and participated in many group shows. She maintains a busy teaching and lecture schedule, both nationally and internationally. For the past 23 years, she has conducted quilt retreats near her island home in northern Michigan. She was a regular columnist for *Lady's Circle Patchwork Quilts* for 12 consecutive years and continues to write for many quilt magazines. *Gwen Marston's Needlework Designs* is her nineteenth book, and her sixth with AQS.

# Other Books by the Author

Marston, Gwen. *Classic Four-Block Appliqué Quilts: A Back-to-Basics Approach.* Lafayette, CA: C&T Publishing, Inc., 2005.

_____. *Fabric Picture Books.* Paducah, KY: American Quilter's Society, 2002.

_____. *Liberated Quiltmaking.* Paducah: KY: American Quilter's Society, 1997.

_____. *Liberated String Quilts: 20 Foundation-Free Projects.* Lafayette, CA: C&T Publishing, Inc., 2003.

_____. *Mary Schafer, American Quilt Maker.* The University of Michigan Press, 2004. (Recipient of Michigan Library 2005 Notable Book Award)

_____. *Q is for Quilt.* Michigan State University Press, 1987.

_____. *Twenty Little Amish Quilts.* Dover Publications, 1993.

_____. *Twenty Little Four Patch Quilts.* Dover Publications, 1996.

_____. *Twenty Little Log Cabin Quilts.* Dover Publications, 1995.

_____. *Twenty Little Pinwheel Quilts.* Dover Publications, 1994.

_____. *Twenty Little Triangle Quilts.* Dover Publications, 1997.

Marston, Gwen and Joe Cunningham. *70 Classic Quilting Patterns: Ready-to-Use Designs and Instructions.* Dover Publications, 1987.

_____. *American Beauties: Rose and Tulip Quilts.* Paducah, KY: American Quilter's Society, 1988.

_____. *Amish Quilting Patterns: Full-size Ready-to-Use Designs and Complete Instructions.* Dover Publications, 1987.

_____. *Mary Schafer and Her Quilts.* Michigan State University Press, 1990.

_____. *Quilting with Style: Principles for Great Pattern Designs.* Paducah, KY: American Quilter's Society, 1993.

_____. *Sets and Borders.* Paducah, KY: American Quilter's Society, 1987.

_____. *Twenty Little Patchwork Quilts.* Dover Publications, 1990.

# Other AQS Books

This is only a small selection of the books available from the American Quilter's Society. AQS books are known worldwide for timely topics, clear writing, beautiful color photos, and accurate illustrations and patterns. The following books are available from your local bookseller, quilt shop, or public library.

#6903      us$19.95

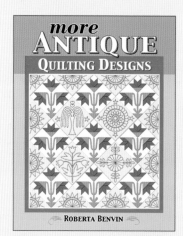

#6907      us$21.95

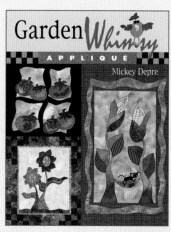

#6904      us$21.95

#6897      us$22.95

#6002      us$15.95

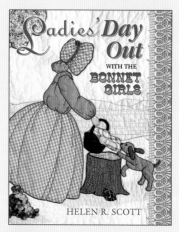

#6676      us$22.95

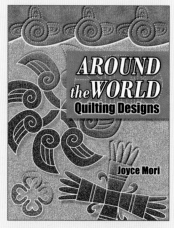

#6806      us$21.95

#6797      us$22.95

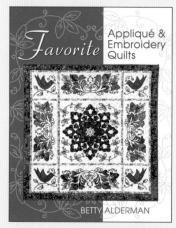

#6410      us$19.95

**Look** for these books nationally.
**Call** or **Visit** our Web site at

# 1-800-626-5420
## www.AmericanQuilter.com